WE ARE CHANGED
TO DEER
AT THE
BROKEN PLACE

Kelly Weber

KELLY WEBER (she/they) holds an MFA
from Colorado State University and is
the author of the chapbook *The Dodo
Heart Museum* (dancing girl press,
2021). Their work has received Pushcart
nominations and has appeared or is
forthcoming in *The Laurel Review*,
Brevity, *The Missouri Review*, *Cream
City Review*, *Palette Poetry*, *Southeast
Review*, *Passages North*, and elsewhere.
She lives in Colorado with two rescue
cats. More of their work can be found at
kellymweber.com.

"The irony of Kelly Weber's brilliant first book of poetry is how sexy each sentence feels pressed to tongue. This is a book obsessed with sound, with the haunting creak of animals breaking through human bodies, canter and flight. Sex is everywhere in this book, and romance, too. And yet the lived experience Weber captures is Aroace Girl, aromantic and asexual, attached to the natural world but refusing expected couplings. She slithers, untethered; she claws, shoots, bleeds in a landscape described with such heartbreakingly beautiful precision that we're forced to question what sex is, anyway. What is a body without another body pressed against it, inside it, stealing its dreams? Who is this Aroace Girl who stands so confidently in the sights of the hunter, knowing she doesn't need anything in her mouth but words, anything between her legs but an arrow she shoots from her thighs? She's magic. This book is stunning, like nothing else, and so sure of its experience that it won't be bullied or twisted into submitting to norms: of hetero, of couple, of labor. Every poem feels original, unsettling, starkly refusing to bend to the cishet world's will. I listened to the body in wonder. I let words escape me again and again."

—*CAROL GUESS, AUTHOR OF* GIRL ZOO *AND* DOLL STUDIES: FORENSICS

The staggering beauty of these poems lies in their ability to re-envision what the body, & a life, might be capable of. Weber deftly transforms experience into landscapes that the speaker can daughter, even desperately, as sky or a deer or struck iron, to be visible. The poems give shape and form to the concerns of asexuality and aromanticism, *'concluding asexuality is not a disorder / but a distinct orientation,'* as the speaker asks in different ways over the course of the collection, 'how can I want / my skeleton to hold you / with softness I don't have.' The movement from 'the entrance of the body' to 'beautiful' might be perilous, yet it proves worthwhile, as is entering this stunning book, 'headwatered in these bodies of ours,' where to enter means to allow language to translate dying into living into "a river too full to contain all this sky."

—*CHELSEA DINGMAN, AUTHOR OF* THROUGH A SMALL GHOST *AND* THAW

WE ARE CHANGED TO DEER AT THE BROKEN PLACE

Kelly Weber

Tupelo Press
North Adams, Massachusetts

ISBN-13: 978-1-946482-80-8

Library of Congress LCCN: 2022034815
Library of Congress Cataloging-in-Publication Data available on request.

Cover and text design by Kenji Liu.
Cover image: "The Thought of Thinking." Bear Kirkpatrick, 2015. Used by permission of the artist.

First paperback edition December 2022

Tupelo Press
P.O. Box 1767
North Adams, Massachusetts 01247
(413) 664-9611 / Fax: (413) 664-9711
editor@tupelopress.org / www.tupelopress.org

Tupelo Press is an award-winning independent literary press that publishes fine fiction, non-fiction, and poetry in books that are a joy to hold as well as read. Tupelo Press is a registered 501(c)(3) non-profit organization, and we rely on public support to carry out our mission of publishing extraordinary work that may be outside the realm of the large commercial publishers. Financial donations are welcome and are tax deductible.

TABLE OF CONTENTS

ASEXUAL

3 b: not having sexual feelings toward others : not experiencing sexual desire or attraction

AROMANTIC

having little or no romantic feeling toward others : experiencing little or no romantic desire or attraction

——MERRIAM-WEBSTER.COM

WHAT THE WATER BRUISES INTO

And sometimes at night when I want to bed down in my mother's bones again I return to that place when I was small, all my friends living luminous and afraid in their mothers' houses, when the cop in sex ed class told us *and if a girl says no but doesn't pull away, resist her or she'll try to accuse you of rape*—when his hips bouquet pelvis and gun—when the room is filled with breath clenched in rib—when I step this close to the entrance of the body again, remember this like the story my mother told me of the man who broke the wall with fist above her head, and I the egg lodging its tiny axe inside her—when again in the dark room they project the coarse-haired babies grown like deer children in the bellies of those who trespassed, the vaginas punished with disease; when we ask forgiveness and mothers turn away—when I swear I didn't know this way back to binding my dangerous body again and here I am anyway, this rope of hair and ice around my wrists, kneeling before this law of white gravel, rattlesnakes hung on fences, flatirons' canted breasts on the edge of glaciers' work—when January is buried among the yearlings, when all you can think of, like me, is this testament of a single white bulb above your tongue finding a way to say what your love is made of, gasoline clear as daylight—then let this be something good; and if she says yes, praise her; and if she says no, praise her too; and if she's followed home in the dark, let her find her way safe or open her mouth wide as night; let the language of prairie dropseed and little bluestem, in all their asexual beauty, give her the term for what she is before she knows; let her find again the truck sunk in the lake inside her, cross the vertebrae of ice in street, lock the bathroom door, lay down the god's arrows carried so long, run hot water in the tub until clouds cover even the doe skull on the counter—and if you're like me and reaching for mothers inside the wind, wanting someone to hold your body beautiful, then enter into the work this way—find your quiver, let your hand slide down to the place all life begins, touch with such praise what they taught you was trap: this slicked apse, this winter harnessed at the wide singing of these double-lipped doors, this dawn yawning black boning deep in your body, this ache of each knuckle circling faster and faster in your second mouth, spitting your name and cradling a whole new creature between your legs, crying clean and clear to the blue mountains ringed with snow, your own voice saying *yes yes yes*—

I

"…she wished she had her arrows handy—
but making do with what she had, scooped up
water and flung it in Actaeon's face…"

—OVID, *THE METAMORPHOSES*, III.232-239,
TRANSLATION BY CHARLES MARTIN

"She would bring down the little birds.
And I would bring down the little birds.
…
I tread my mother's wrist and would draw blood."

—ROBERT DUNCAN, "MY MOTHER WOULD BE A FALCONRESS"

GOLD SHYNESS (WITH LINES FROM ANNE CARSON)

I look at the target and men look
at me. Every breathing cage

of ribs locked. How often have I been someone's
competition, aligned in this field?

Once I watched a man bury
himself in a wooden coffin just to prove he could

hold his breath longer than the others.
Thin lines of force coordinate

between arm, string, moon—frame
to hang this burning on.

The figure is a triangle. In the bow, perfection
of the tree killed to make it.

Young men swirl dead wasps in a jar
and tell me it's honey.

*Oh the things I could
sonnetize you with.* My hips

a cow skull tipped upside down, spilling
pink blossoms from the broken fossa.

I could line up all the holes in my days
and shoot through them

but in the end all the men
would be dead on the floor. No glamor in what's easy.

You can name hunger whatever you want
and still it won't belong to you.

I'll dip the shaft in my own red,
let its fletching strike the thin skin

over my radius and ulna on release: hunter's bruise.
Broken set of stitches across the cream

field before us, the arrow quivering in the eye
of the bull, blood rising to meet it.

ABSTINENCE

I am one of the good girls.
Boys come back to school with new rodeo buckles
and like any good girl I admire the hips
circled in the silver hooves of bucking broncos.
I bleed discretely. I cry properly
when a girl drowns in the dam's lake. The boys winch a doe
out of the water and gut it, read the pink coil
of viscera and plastic for a hint
of how many throats they'll conquer.
My mother tells to resist temptation
and I wonder which temptation she means,
what allure a jawline holds for me.
Boys flick paper footballs at my face
to see it hit with white
and I keep sewing a needle through my palm.
Like the moth I am mistaken for helpless
and like the moth I orient by the light by another gravity.
Sometimes boys drive out to fields to shoot
something living. I have no word for aroace.
In the kitchen I wait at the door
for laughing fathers to swell the sky.
My mother gave me a scorpion sealed under glass.
Something to teach me about learning to contain
what is dangerous.
I press my palms to the window, following
another storm blowing in: Durango,

Telluride, Rifle, Creede, every name I give

to knobs of my body. Everyone tethers their thrashing

to each other's honey-dark pupils.

Mothers use us as warning, point to bare shoulders,

drag us again before the altar.

Try not to be seen.

Trust no one, even friends, who may betray

me to men. When boys ask in class

if I want to hold hairy balls in my mouth, I bow my head

until they can't help but admire me.

The worst thing possible does not happen to me.

I'm a good girl. I drive a nail into the wall

for each bit of iron I've distilled from blood

threaded from my fingers. People think it's a cross

but it's my spine I've tacked above the bed.

I resist eating a single seed of that red pomegranate

of my furious heart, or I might just throw over hell

and clasp his bone crown to name myself queen.

I leave the window open too long at night.

Winter rain cinches my navel silver.

WHEN I LEARNED TO BE FOURTEEN

the first time I didn't want to dance with him but I did anyway, linked arms around his sweaty neck, passing as best I could. the song ossified & broke on the coda. *you love him* the dancers said. *no* I wanted to say but rings filled my mouth. his mother saying *you'd be so good for him* I was shaking my head *I want to be a huntress.* he unfastened my pelvis & called it *honey-lovely,* cradled it gently beneath him, so I grew an aspen out of each hole, one single twin organism beating its clone-pluralled hearts. everyone said *she's young.* he leaned to my mouth so I hardened my spit to *fuck you.* everyone said *bitch.* I ran. each time I stopped a man wanting to be something better clung to my body, thrust in and arched back until he split right through his skin, left his carapace dangling while he buried the song he grew in me below ground. I tried to be girl again each time, soften husk, but I had to snap a root, bleed a little more, peel bark from phalanges, leave a tongue in silence and spittle.

take the bow that would've hunted, try to make a sternum of it. tensile enough not to break. the story repeats: all of us tree girls learned to be of : of rib, of run, of gaze, of gone, of pursuit, of shatter. spiled in a crowd, where everyone could see. *he had a swan's tender neck, he earned it. he shed his bull body to become a boy for me* everyone said. *he was golden showers of rain in mouth, soft enough to be owed something.* one gave birth in sweet-sticky sap, bloodgold welling from her bulging side after hours to a baby that—shame, we said—cried only branches from its mouth. we've tried to still ourselves invisible. small light. zeroed on the mirror our breath, drawn words in it. men want our lips gasp-widened on glass & wreath us round their heads, tether us to fourteen here making us the hunter's crown we'd have worn. self-named gods, they swagger, see ass, hear ace, know they can correct that, want girls on the cusp of beg & green, light locked so deep only they can harvest & haul it up.

WHERE THE SKY'S MILK COMES IN

You want to return to that year of cats
   and autumn, that place where prairie
      is ghost hair roping up to brush the surface

of cornfields, condoms crumpled pearls
   down the middle of town's one road, buzzards
      spiraled on sky bled from the slaughterhouse

and its men. That was the season of hungering
   into shy hips and the cats who kept giving birth,
      poaching refuse and dragging swollen bellies

to the teenage boys who fed them, slat-ribbed
   and cratered in acne, coming into the soft bones
      of their bodies and offering scabbed knuckles to

ferals before they were men. That was the season
   when the cats were given secret offerings of tuna
      with arsenic on porches, and all the boys grew quiet

in their fathers' houses, looking at the deer
   with milk-thin legs hanging off the edge
      of another year, breath tightened to covenant—

and the season, too, of girls
   and the boys who happened to them,
      the girl who stood at the lip of the reservoir—when you

think that if you just walked back long enough
   you'd find them there again, your knees
      fringed in the pale harmonies

of katydids and grass stinging open
   into so much light it lets the summer go in blades
      and you could wade to a boy in the dark stable

of his father leaning his head against a mare's flank
          to weep where August pearls tighter and tighter
                    where silence would open to you again.

EVERYONE REMEMBERS THEIR FIRST TIME

First time I bump a girl's hip and it breaks into red-
winged blackbird, I have to walk out
of the barn dance and to the silo, unmooned
and full of carbon black or seed—I can't tell—
brace my forehead on such ribbed
silver, trembling at how
our pelvis both grieves and dawns,
how a cry-loosened femur twists on a blood tether
of feather and blue vein, how I want to kick
and crawl inside that unsocketed
heart at the same time, weeping together—
what a fierce life I've lived since.

REASONS I WOULDN'T BE A GOOD MOTHER

1. I'm a blue dog skull with a hole drilled in it. 2. Virga snow over a city of tongues. 3. That is, my body is an unsafe home meant only for extremophiles, subspecies of one. 4. Or something like that. 5. Because when I was a child my mother sat on the hood of the car and taught me to throw oranges we couldn't afford to the gas station ravens. 6. Because what I learned of love I learned from her hands. 7. Pith from rind, citrus and husk. 8. Night's indigo cloak opens over the mountain city and her bleeding heart drips slag from the welding crews working all through her hours. 9. Because men want women to be mothers and want mothers to have no children. 10. Because I have had to teach myself to daughter and be kind to my body first. 11. Because selfishness is a learned survival trait like cutting things out of the self: self-hatred, desire for male attention, submission. 12. When I was a child I parted the lips of my pussy in the shallows of Blue Mesa reservoir and looked at my clitoris through water and fish, and already knew what I did not want to make of it. 13. Every baby doll's hollow clicking plastic head with unsleeping eyes. 14. Everyone's opinion on this. 15. Because mine matters least. 16. Blood-borne rifles churning through my belly's church calcifying under lake. 17. People guess they understand why someone wouldn't want to bring a child into this. 18. Swallows who follow me down the street can't smell the hands that took their children. 19. Because I could be a mother. 20. With a cracked bowl for a belly and a scream hissing out of her heart. 21. Because I would hate myself and hate her for it. 22. Because I could be good too. 23. Maybe I would take her to see the museum's chromolithographs of the national parks a hundred years ago, show her the blues and the browns of Yosemite and Sangre de Cristo and Grand Prismatic Spring burned there with acid and water until all that was left on the stone and the paper were the colors the earth once was. 24. Tell her she needs to be river and mud, acid that etches something permanent onto men's tongues. 25. Perhaps I'd teach us both to drown. 26. Maybe what I've really learned to mother inside myself is grieving.

27. Sometimes I look at the street frozen over and start weeping for no good reason at all. 28. Because I harden like milk and soften like graupel. 29. Because sometimes I just want to know that I'm capable of such strength to push a whole world through my pelvis and have it be made of something in me even if I never want the after. 30. Truth is the real genesis story wasn't a rib but a person who saw all the other animals exhausted from trying to survive all day and said yeah, me too, and broke off pieces of her bones to give to them so at least they could all share in it. 31. Because I dream that I lower myself in a cage to the bottom floor of an abortion clinic where they cradle my body through its blood and afterward dress me in paper and help me to sleep. 32. That's not even a poem that's just the truth. 33. Because mother bone and pearl. 34. Because every sharp thing overflows. 35. Because God's a pebble in the mouth you suck to make saliva to keep from dying of thirst. 36. That is, even God must fall on his knees and answer if I bring him here before me. 37. That is, even a huntress who helped her mother birth must stop at a bar at the end of the day. 38. I nurse with such blood. 40. But hush, still: I take you in my jaws; I gentle you with tongue. 39. I will teach each thing I birth to know its way out, to make its escape. 40. When there is no escape be like water—what makes an escape fast enough to make a canyon or a chamber, heart or bullet. 41. I mean make a way out that keeps you alive. 42. I mean to raise each thing against my belly to kill.

LITTLE SONG, QUICKENING

a cry clean as a coffin at the party everyone softly
competes to hold the baby and I cannot make
myself feel this rain glazes the glass they are saying
my pretty girl my pretty girl a soft pink eucharist face
crumbling on the boat we can see the shadows of
fish on the sonar branches poking above the lake's
shore I touch my lips am I a woman am I femme
enough if I don't want small bones pressed against
my chest on land the fontanelle forest is gray &
stripped of bark by deer everyone wants to hold the
thing in my chest a doe unfolds its hooves hold me
steady if she breaks loose she can't swim neither of
us can I can be as small as a baby's fourteen-inch box

ANCHOR POINT, ARROW SAW

I wake with the fist
of my heart's iambs knocking my mother's voice

hissing like a box of nails hitting floor, another year
falling to the ground. Sky hardtack and

ice cracking. Her breasts
pressed against my back. We are surrounded

by our mothers' voices first
in that breathing that is not drowning

yet. She is trying to tell me how to daughter: escape
and hands. Tell me how to make a way out

of rage, of this strange shedding
housed inside my hips. Tell me there's a way to be anything

but what we were taught, quiet
blades we buried under the dirt

kneeling before men's mouths. I rise
to the window, graft my palms

to glass and frost. The stars arrive
from their deaths and behind the daylight.

Tell me this is the way to be strong,
dancing naked and blindfolded

with indigo on an empty bed, water climbing
above my pubis mons, the oxygen line

of first wound I trace with both hands.
Copperheads I was taught to name on sight

coiling around my thighs, each pink mouth
a satin casket lined with teeth pearled

with hemorrhage, thimbles of wine
and wafer where we fall to our knees again.

NUPTIAL BONES

We pale into a veil of skin over knobs, my neck
   bows beneath yours, your hips coupled to mine

shafts beneath us. Deer cry softly. You clutch a bed of this pelvis
   for yourself and I don't want to want this—your brute attention, licking

my name, claiming I was made for you, of you. I was taught to want more
   than my own self, my worth a rare skeleton sunk in the reservoir

of the body that breath wraps around itself, enduring
   until rupture. Your weight steepled between my thighs. First

light frosting this bed. Dawn chorus plucking pink strings
   of rattlesnake flesh littering the porch. It's hard not to be straight

-backed, not to want the gaze I've been raised to love, to resist
   this worship of your thousand mouths on me—all of you demanding

I yield to the good hunger I should be. I swear blue
   hours into this four-chambered oath, a vow to keep

in rib. A trailed gown of blackbirds startling, every feather a nail
   in a house I cannot see yet.

SOFT OBEDIENCE

Late morning rain breaks with horses
still hitched for trail too muddy to ride—

untethered from posts and soft obedience, they
shy against each other, dark eyes not holding us

circling corral and nipping flanks
roped with lather like god's semen

until gate swings and they ripple into as one wheel of lungs.

I wonder what it would take to hurt you
if I were your lover, how deep my thumb could press

your throat to make you cry—perhaps I know enough
to know this is a mercy

to not be able to harm this way, you and I
walking without bones touching, where wind remembers

bluestem into water beneath all the animals touching faces.

NORTH OF HELL

                    Say I can still be kind here, in this place we've made
of our blood and bone. That I can be the good child
                    though I've too often been afraid, buried this sunrise

of my breath behind my sternum and cinched my black coat tight,
                    kept walking by the river where the ice cratered
beneath her bones. In seasons like this certain men tire

                    of ace folks like me who deny them what they're
owed. They trade pictures of her body
                    after she's dead, say this is what happens to the ones

who withhold. I try to hold her in my mind, see her standing
                    like this at the edge of the ice-bound river
raising her head, a doe for each one of us like her who is gone.

                    Say that on the other side of such rupture, perhaps,
there can be this necessary transformation, a lifting into something
                    that knows only the clean thirst of trees. That even

ash can be undone. Say there's still a way to hold this last indigo light
                    with gentleness. Say that it falls across the chapel
of December trees, that the stars I clutch

                    aren't just a girl's hair.
Say I'm someone hooking to whatever
                    cold meridian I can find, this far west and north

of what we once called beautiful. On this bare floor
                    of high desert, I stand among the deer—
their breaths kneel about me, antlers bowed

                    a field of moving bone.

II

NOCTURNE WITH AROACE GIRL

What pulls a person like me
out here alone, they want to know? What heartbreak am I
running from where coyote eyes and yellow coneflowers sting
the black? I steer the moon over my right shoulder, vertebrae
lodged above coyote ridge, winding plains road.
I drive all the night's hungers down, white light
clasping the devil's backbone. Today snow blanked
the mountains and their highway beneath me.
Prairie of cancellous bone, prayer of distance
and homes. Not heartbreak but a way to let the clotted
salt crow of joy out of my throat. Pulse flicker,
how quick to keep up with thirst. Shame is not
a god I'll bow to anymore. Dilate shale's radio song.
Strip sorrow from the larynx. Not broken
but igneous. Glutted with night
and everything that lives within it and me.
Nothing is alone while it still has breath enough
to survive on something else. Half rib
and half name—I'm arched cervix and wheel glitter,
headlights cinched to a cow skull's absent tongue.
I want to be remembered as a little snap between teeth
hungering for the next heart. I will not be bound to day
or bed, bright veils and myths of how to be lonely. I am full
of so many things remaining past body: shadow trailing
a skeleton a behind it, a voice laughing past the reach
of men who hunt a small thing's escape.
Tell me I want to fuck all you
want. I'm mothered by gnaw and moth, yawned rapturous
in obliterate dark. A few houses scattered
marrow in the sage. I spill my guts in dirt
to read my future minute to minute. Tell me
my throat was made for swallowing one thing only.
Watch my jaws open wide and pink where all small things
are hunted, make a dawn of teeth and meadowlark song.

AROACE GIRL WITH KETTLES AND CRADLES

I make space for everyone and for every man's anger

like lead in milk I know how to be invisible even to myself

come morning I'll be human again

but tonight I'm unchurched jawbone chewing sulphur from

a match for every time I've smiled in spite of

I shut out the mouths of everyone who wants

to feed from whatever teat they can find on me

I bow in a kitchen fulminated to such unfamiliar light

I tear my lips off so no words soften

my spine to salt—I slide my hand down to cradle

every name for the extinction I pull from between my thighs

loving no one but myself

I am so unconscionable

a heart boils in the belly of every kettle screaming like a baby

I will arrange all my locks

of hair on the floor and call them my periods

severed from the ends of sentences for people

all I've grown just to cut away

AROACE GIRL WITH TRAPS

the first time I moved alone between empty walls & unboxed the contents of my life friends said they missed the
spare years when they lived without & hungering for another in their bed & before the baby's small bones &
when I came here the sink water kept electrocuting me mildly as any penitent angel & the space under the stairs
was full of empty pill bottles & a friend's mother came to hang a cross on the wall & say the pain of being single
is not forever & say I'll pray for you until & I found steel wool stuffed in the outlet under the sink & the previous
owner tried to keep out the small hungers of mice after her husband died & I live with the teeth I've inherited in
a house with room enough to fit more & the couple next door fight & fuck beneath the mounted deer head & I
fashion a pair of lungs from my breath on the window & find a mouse the cats killed & licked the skull clean & I
set traps & remember when I walked through the slats of an unfinished house & wrote my name on wood in red ink
& lighting white candle litanies wondering how to stave off death without a body to push me down & I try to read
a love poem the most universal thing & someone said the ampersand looks like a pregnant belly & I wake in dark
backs cracking in half

AROACE GIRL'S PETITION

and it's true sometimes / someone looks at me asking nothing / and I want that face
cupped between my palms / a door hinged open / with a gray severed wing rocking in it
/ I saw once walking into my office / and its small brick rooms / everything that tethers /
twisting red from that bare knob of bone / a whole series of inward knots / I hold in my
hands / and it's true I've never broken up with anyone / never let anyone kiss my jaw into
a riot of thistle / a ring of dark-eyed junco and barbed wire / I'm bound to / never been
that hell across a throat / but sometimes I want to sit with someone's wrists / between my
knees pearl / their pulse with eggs from the fallen wasp nest / drowned in a honeycomb
of spit and bark / the work of such careful attention / and days / I used to tend an ashbed
where the excavated skeletons / of ancient deer and horses sprawled / bellies torn open
by dogs and birth canals / tangled with small bones / they wanted to keep close / I have
tried to commit a life to such bright forgetting / of the many fractures I've asked blessed /
again and again the rattlesnakes crushed on highway / shadow of a train strutted across
my body / hauling blades to wind farms toothed and bleached / like the maw of some
lost ichthyosaur / and yes it's true / I want / to bless the water broken / to make one
more day to live / on raw / gasoline and looking at someone who trusts / their softness
to my breathing / in the spaces we share / I get it / dying for someone I mean / I'll
always want to tug their dark coat / tighter press my forehead to theirs against wind say
/ goddamn / before they walk into snow / remove a bone too soon / and it bruises the
memory of water / from the ground

AROACE GIRL : PLAINSONG ELEGY

this is how I find you huddled, false boneset and
rocking against wall with your tongue
ringing winter air. this is how we kneel
of a single sky's unsnowing. this is how I draw
morning cleaved at the marrow. you loved him
a lover. virgin, spinster, frigid, maid, failed
still gripped by osprey, windbreak, pinewood.
where we come from
—there is no way to grieve the loss of
in wait for the words for what we were. this is
front, freeze coming across plains, the blades
—let's take the roads of winter's throat again
from a no-trespassing sign, hand it to you
like a coneflower, the way you told me
it's the strongest weapon there is:
listening to our breaths,
panic grass and the wind gathered to fill

antelope horn clenched in your fist,
locked in the white bell of your skull
at the broken spot, undone by downstroke
you into the circle of my bones, blue
—say it, you loved him even if you're not
straight. this is how we're bound by prairie—
this is how we find no revelation in death—
girls don't cry, they weather
a friend so fully, the years we spent lying
how we let ourselves feel it
in your shoulders exposed and shaking.
and I can pluck an antler crowned in snow
as a bouquet. you can fold a dictionary page
at your sister's wedding, making this,
thirst. the meadow we come home to
finding no solace in his gone,
this smaller circle we make together

AUBADE WITH AROACE GIRL

moon falls   a jawbone toward the ridge   bruising new snow across the backs
of mountains named   for blood of a sacrifice   I stand at the edge of cliff
every flake stinging open   tongues of cholla and saguaro cutting white-dusted
crosses against horizon's dark shaft of spur   and basin down below   in my
pelvis   the widest part of the female body   grief too lives   the narrow dusks
of timber   each lavender shadow in the desert   something I've mothered in
me   when they tell me   I don't exist   I make a thin stirrup against cloud   my
black shirt clasped against my pink collarbone   and I say exist   and cutthroat
trout pour their silver back into the stream   I say exist and the horses come
back   to their soft faces in the bed of a lake that made them   exist and the
long-gone river and its bones fill my chest   here in cavity and spire   in angel
shale and canyon I come here to name   every cloven-hoofed animal   that
beds down in dust   this center of sunrise   is tooth and throat   I watch
over every half-sleeping creature   shiver-eyed dark as the space between stars
listening for sharp-mawed hungers hunting them   I clutch this whole line of
mountains to my clavicle   chert and shale   open my hip and all this will cry
out   a word   am I not animal enough for you if I do not want   the same
as everyone else   if you peel back this flesh and this sternum   blue-cavitied
and wet-ventricled   am I not this heart's struggle to survive   fast-beating
with the cold   and your touch   thirsty as a rattlesnake   that awakens after
the long warm nest of bodies around it all season   am I not a muscle   trying to
hold every minute open   isn't sky our first attempt to reach   a body that isn't
ours   to hold   come here and rest   inside me I will keep the muzzles at bay
I will offer scrap and carcass   something to endure another night   every
glisten point grommet black sky   I will be what you pray toward   my throat
a churchyard of cactus all us extinct beasts sleeping   every ventricle pushing
blood   toward morning   pale of my wrists enough to keep us   whole set in
dawn's hard dark

AROACE GIRL, LEVEED

You stand over me, water
running from your antlers and breasts.

I offer you my belly, the prairie rattler
coiled in my uterus, dropseed

blue grama and little bluestem locked
tight in its mouth against extinction.

You cloud a morning out of this place
born smooth as any grave.

It's okay to weep in front of people—I tell myself
even the rock you gave me from the Colorado

for my birthday was granite opened and hammered
with clavicle, limestone, truckbed

and gutshot. Once I rocked shut to any soft word.
A crib by the side of the highway

of ribs slatted to wind. All my life
I've been running from that treeless cold,

yoked to plains and a winter woman's
refusal to cry, to fold into threaded scrap

of tire shrapnel. I sucked a dead quail's feathers in my mouth.
What I shed, I shed gladly. Touch my shoulders

and I'll release all my grief at once
the way slabs of ice migrate

under chords of stars over roads
after prairie floods. You lean over me

and weep, afraid of what
we are. I tell you we are those animals

driven desperate by hunger to cross
a river too full to contain all this sky.

SKIN HUNGER

I must confess: I live with the headless torso of a man.
By night I sleep against his chest. By day I spit

on his name and bury him three times in my chest.
I laugh too loudly when people ask

if I'm lonely. At parties I slip my voice
in the armature of his empty ribs and hum to drown

out all the noise. At home I make a blood spiral
of myself. I tell him to trace the line of my back in moonlight

and he makes a lye-constellated scorpion. A raven perches
in the window clutching a jacaranda berry in its beak.

One each night for each thing I've chewed from my wrist
and each person I've pushed away who wanted to love

me without body or question. I touch-
starve myself into such a naked shape. If anyone knocked

on my door right now I'd walk around the lake
slowly with my hair on fire, bury all the lights in water.

UNDER THE SNOWS OF JUNE

this month isn't for ace/aro identities and never will be. shut the fuck up. —aphobeasriel, tumblr post

I can't seem to find the bottom
        of my larynx—I keep going until I hit ice sheet
glacier turquoised inside this gullet's mountain
        cave. This is the month I was born

and each year I try to do it again, pulling myself
        through your hands, Mother—
quarrying out of cervix the hardest water
        and daughter cells. I can't stop saying

I don't deserve things, I should give up every space I breathe.
        Down here every syllable booms hysterical,
catches between my teeth like a red egg
        that's my inheritance of stone.

If I don't give birth to a daughter,
        will the rage passed from mother to mother harden
in me, wind refrained to a hell's gate?
        Mother please braid my hair

though I cut it off years ago.
        You and my father
setting an entire ticking season
        in my wrist, building a heart out of blue

and a good fuck I'll never know. If I bury the head
        of a match in this ice, will it go on burning
in slow motion, swallowed like a dead horse
        clattering the sparks of its hooves?

I try to find pride in the ridged palate
        of my mouth, in the oxygen cratering this roof

of words, in this stalagmite's patient falling upward.
      It's so easy to feel eroded. It's so easy to feel broken in such yawns

of entire silences spreading—
      it's hard to feel that I'm real, to speak.
Every fissure a lapsed choir under the cirque
      pitched so far above, chandeliered chewing of my own damned tongue.

DERMATILLOMANIA

Up the canyon carved from angel shale, I carry my little pulse
of wind into the hole of a rock-cut basin, tethering my breath
to the abandon of the wrecked car I crawl inside and to the dark
of the river's torque chewing the red and purple littoral.

Winding my breath in the washbasin of my chest, I cut each tether
and count the acetylene trees, one crooked paling for each of my sins.
I am riven from the water's red chewing.
I cry into the steering wheel. Abandoned antlers in the backseat

strew snapped shadows of branches on the window glass, crooks
to lead me to a kind of mercy. Bowing, I bite each of my fingers
and pull back the skin, a wheel's cry like rubbing velvet from antlers
one for each fear—part punishment, part distraction.

I've tried tying bows, but each ribbon clinches to a silken bite.
So I tear the same scrap loose from each nail's bed: the index
finger pointing to a future punishment sure to fall, one hope
I've severed from another. Ring finger for each time I've hooked

myself to something I shouldn't have—this index's bed of nails
hidden in my back—and thumb for the things I've said
that sank a ring of hooks in another. Pinky bone, what I refused
to let myself think about this week. Middle finger, this dirty secret

I've kept hidden from others, said I didn't it need to live. How
amazing, to watch my skin forgive me, to be shucked clean as midwinter
to myself thinking in bone and secret, to pinked dirt and blessed
frost-awed and hungered in the car's skeleton drown

in winter's rivered sound. Forgive my skin's scarring,
forgive what I refuse to name this. It's so hard to believe I'm good,
thirst absolved in moon's blue, hunger-awed in my frosted skeleton
speaking each hand bone: lunate, capitate, winding sheet.

ORIENTING (WITH LINES FROM NADIA NOOREYEZDAN)

you told me once   we would let snow approach
             us in the forest

and when I wait   green-gowned and barefoot for IV
             again I think of the lungs

singing in the branches   of the bitter berry tree
             hundreds of mountain chickadees dropping

silent then opening   all at once
             a systole of wings in cold

we were just starting to feel   when you told me
             you weren't attracted to anyone either

can't sound this vein   the nurse says the one
             who does this painlessly is hunting a buck

gone widening   every gap in my pulse they tell me
             my tongue

will numb before his hands   open my sleep my body
             this body this counting

backwards they   say my hearing will leave
             last and I number

every ringneck   every northern flicker you
             still know every kind

dark and how to be   home when even these small
             labors exhaust every bruise

a small hungry mouth *paper* *concluding asexuality is not a disorder*
             but a distinct orientation how can I want

my skeleton to hold you   with softness I don't have
                                                    ache for evenings weighed

under blanket & indigo   I ring my sick innards
                                                    beneath pines I call this desire

to love you just this much   to break
                                                    when we

make a ceremony   of my body devouring itself

FIBRILLATIONS FOR COFFIN ICE

What a trick, this growing a mirror
inside me—a circle of men calling

me capable, how I pass this last test
in the house of rage and dust to prove myself, bearing

silver so pure in my body, arching
backward on a table full of arsenic-

seeded apples and water from a dead horse
lake. Hair spools from every spigot

in this kitchen. *Don't you want to be the strongest weapon?*
Yes, yes, I am trying to say beneath the sawed-off

cliff they place across my mouth, the lines
of sugar and granite they crumble across

my belly to lick whiskey from my navel.
My shoulder blades hinge into a blank

black prairie and every word I hook
out of bluestem gets lost on the way to tongue.

Now they have opened the hole in my stomach
wide enough to pour in mare's milk, pull

out the things they say I should shed and will
have no further use for: intestine, uterus, nucleus accumbens.

Don't make space for anyone. When I think I've done
it they tell me to push against their hands

until I can keep them away, so I weather my spine
into a bridge of sandstone threaded with screws, muscle

their palms off my sutured middle, but when I look up
between my thighs the room is empty—

down the hall another man's crowning
a ring of dull noise. I rise, crouch at the keyhole where

they've gone to applaud, whisper what's left of my blood
I could rust to salt and shatter, crying such iron.

CROWN OF SCREWS

with her hands between my legs she asks / if I want to keep
going / on her shoulder a blue hawk / plunges cobalt nickel and
beryllium ink into / the little card of faces this nurse handed me
to ask / how often have you been feeling this way this clear / loop
of face crying / I pointed to / my face why are you sad she asked
/ I can't stop all this salt / pouring out of my skull I / can't stop
double-breathing the circle of uterus / dancing above my head
the poster of menstrual cycle / egg sliding down tube to / land
how long does it take to make skin permanent how long does it /
hold memory of hands pressing a needle across / town a crowd
of grandmothers hold signs protesting a judge / what is indelible
in the tough gray matter of the brain do / you use birth control
she is asking no / I'm ace aro my Crohn's medicine is failing or
I'm just / dying these days bear down / she says / bear down it
will hurt less / I weep into her blue-gloved / wings bear down air

*

each day men bring down a new law about my body I scroll
I wing all night through my feed the text on the white crystal
and I am one of the privileged ones I have so little to fear by
comparison I am clicking one law after the next then onto an
auction page for a deer skull the long gray rack tined across
a blonde hardwood floor I keep myself from buying things by
practicing what my counselor taught me trigger the mammalian
dive complex plunging my face into a blue bowl of ice water
make the body think it is drowning and it will try to save itself
forget all other fears I made a bowl like this once not for this
but to teach little kids about earth's atmosphere helping us to
breathe I tried not to think about how one in six of them would
be grabbed by a man's hands that they were breathing air
conceived in a body bone-soft already carbon-fourteened by a
chain of fathers who decided so precisely what would grow in
the body and could never be cut out

*

the speculum is cut from stainless steel with such precise decision
the speculum widens the hole into another word inside them
the speculum has not been replaced with more comfortable forms
the speculum's pain is expected it feels this with a kind of steel light
the speculum finds it normal to experience this to be told no big deal
the speculum thinks a white meadow spewed with screws an engine
the speculum shouldn't hurt and people are disturbed when it doesn't want babies
the speculum flattens a cloud says tits wants the dark red flesh
the speculum rasps winter's chords into a kiss a hawk's stoop
the speculum thinks of itself as a dominant subject position
the speculum can reveal bad cells especially for those who are chronic
the speculum is desert hinge widening pale violet cliff in inner lobes
the speculum staggers after tracks across thin snow in high desert
the speculum just wants to be loved just wants to see be seen wants

*

when she swabs a sample from me I cry harder I want I just want

to go home to a place when my body wasn't afraid wasn't always such

a long slide into zippers and letters a place I mine the iron out of my

blood into teem of wild of thistle of branch of thought of small baby

bones I once was here the air is so waxen and arrhythmic here

I want to slide under the hands of a virgin's cold lead skeleton

headlights to cast my shadows across a road staggered with roadkill chambers nested into mouths gone exquisite with broken bottles

every girl cries when she comes here she is saying between the stirrups

of a pale horse that bears a headless angel on its back wings hollow

boned tipping through cervix gasoline she says yes it's uncomfortable

my friend got cancer on the pill you can get cervical cancer even when

not actively swallowing someone else's drowning if you're anxious if

you're chronic if you live in these skies singed with a crow's thought

*

under my brain's sky it is difficult to singe
new neural pathways. *I feel bad for him he just
made a mistake he's not a bad person just a little
lost.* the lake I lower myself into is a long drop
to mud and fish bones where he says he can hear
me. I push my voice through water to tell him
all the ways he's harmed me and other women
looking at us describing our body
of work. he says *you don't understand me.*
I say *can you just make a little more effort.* he says
he has a hard time with things, begins to weep.
I empathize he goes on weeping antlers pushing
up through my throat and jaw *I'm sorry*
I say but can't around the bone he cries *feel bad for me feel bad for feel bad*

*

feel-bad skin feel-bad hair feel-bad clothes I ask and ask
no it's not uncomfortable it's pain don't unlanguage

this tell myself don't say it's not pain don't say
it's not don't tell yourself to close your legs
and lower your hips into the sink close your legs lower
your hips close your legs lower your hips off the pubic
bone into a shaft of light over horsetooth reservoir the town
flooded down below that can hardly bear
the weight of all that water anymore all the ghosts
that cannot be born but must be must be
each hook saying bear more
bear more
bear more
bear more

*

try imagining the best thing that could happen / more my
counselor says I try / I wake up / tomorrow covered in orioles
each / set of lungs tapping me with their beaks hammering / me
into new song that migrates / toward more tender skies full of
power lines I slide / into them like breath poured / into a herd of
animals running down to the water / to be rid of / pretty baby
pretty baby look at her teeth and how small her / clattering down
the little darknesses / when I walk / out of this exam room I will
not stop weeping for two hours or hurting for two / days must
there always be such daughtering / such slow division of water
and oxygen / split at the forgetting to find a new way to be / to
keep going to find a way to law to live / falling up a way for hands
and legs to keep going

DEVIL'S ROPE, TESTAMENT'S WINTER

I met the deer at their trespass
—I crossed the boundary into
the field. I hungered
that bare gold, kneeling
for any gun to shoot me
for what I thieved in the raw
air of the razed corn. Breath
a tether binding me to that cold
sky gone to star, caught
by everything that sharpened
against my ribs: men's hands
calling me their cunt, forgiveness
for my shivering skin wanting
their praise, mouths
of the dogs I nursed at breasts
of self-hatred and silence to hunt
down others like me.
I came here to be broken in dawn
and its thicket, but not
beneath the knife of a father
to trade for a boy's tremble.
I know how to sever any angel
from its vow, make myself
clean with the unyielding pulse
of my carotid, light jetting
from the harvest
in the four rooms of my chest.
I came to be undone at the word
just downwind of slaughter.
The cut stalks I stole, truth, fire cleft
at the base of lightning's reaping,
trying to carry in my fists
back across a blood-morning wire.

IV

OMPHALOS : TERMED

At the center of the wind I was not born
but cut free. *This is how you be a person*
the world will call a woman my mother told
me. Chewed loose. We nearly died.
Afterwards she held me and in my mouth slipped
coals. I learned to spit up poison
by filling my belly with flammable griefs.
When I was thirteen I remembered the sound
of her downpour and followed to be born again.
She drew circles across my sternum
and said *You can be everything that you are.*
I climbed to the deer stand at the coldest blue hour
and waited for breath to appear. Grace
held in the body, deep in a nine-months' winter
I enter once again.

OMPHALOS : SHORN

My mother learned to mother
from a mother who wished her a boy, cut

her daughter's hair years before I begged mine short.
The first time my mother posed nude

for a woman to paint she found a way
into beautiful. The first time she guided

my father's hand I heard the clock unwind
its teeth, its pendulum the ungrown pulse

of night and all its tongues—broken
surfaces, what we labor forth to light.

OMPHALOS : SINKBOX

after Eduardo Corral

The room smells like blood.
                My grandmother sleeps in a shed with doves,
slaughters chickens. She finds
                the fingerbone of a young woman
when she goes to see where they unearthed
                the body. Cries often into the milk pail
and green heirloom glass.
                Eats nothing but seeds
for years—she breaks in the kitchen
                fine china she sweeps into circles. Rides
a horse through horizon's white line. Raises a hand
                to slap. Uses the horse
to drag home a carburetor from a rotting car
                until the horse drops dead
and she carries home the blue bag of its guts
                a single tibia dragging a hoof in dust.
Knows how to starve a thirst whole.
                Holds her breath underwater.
Climbs onto the table to sway-dance and scream
                at her sister trying to pull her down.
Throws her ring in her face: gold slap. Vanishes
                at herself like this. Kneels for the men. Offers
what she knows she must. Is married
                young. Leaves for days, comes home smelling
of other girls' bones. Arranges on her loom
                the dark. A prayer of blue—
when I am taught years
                later in a state so far from her

crowded with trees

               how to resuscitate someone's breath

I lean over the ragged

               plastic head of a drowned woman, place

my mouth over the cut hole,

               bag for a rib cage, and exhale

until I come up gasping

               these inheritances of fist and wishbone.

OMPHALOS : AIRWASHED

My grandmother listens to her parents through a hole
in the wall, learns how men teach women
to scream. A moon breaks on the tines
of a stag's horns at the end of the field. Nothing

can trick the devil into leaving like an offer of gold.
She gnaws on a horse bridle, softens the leather and brass
against her teeth all night in the chicken coop. What
a man's hand will not take is only for God to know.

She will set a gun on the table between herself
and her daughter. Pick a north and we'll follow. White cow
in the curio cabinet frozen milk. I take their wrists and lead
us in a dance to the four seasons porch, our arms

tugging in our sockets. Once she rode her horse for three days
across a darkened field, past the rut where her sons
were nearly lost and climbed out with old struts of iron,
until she hit the edge of the world in property line and a stop sign.

I'll cut the cow, drain the milk from its hide. I'll take the two
women who made me inside myself and give birth to them
better. Who am I to offer such a thing? My grandmother goes in to
fight her man on the bed and I kneel outside the door, sucking bird bones

like I could put a heart back in each one, feel its rough jumping
inside my mouth. She watches the coyote stealing along the fence
to the coop, the glint of her father's gun taking aim at such hunger.
My mother cups my chin and says she will tell me a story.

OMPHALOS : REVOLVE

I walk down the paneled hallway hung with a line of hens
strung by their feet like guns, their eyes beaded on me

as I walk into my grandmother's bedroom, the blue
comforter trod by a great white peacock who bows her head

and screams for me to never leave. I stand before
the dresser's sleeted mirror, veil my face in a black hair net,

tug at my crooked smile same as hers. I pin a set of pearls
at my neck. This is the bed my mother was daughtered into.

The pillow, the nest of silvering hairs where all the broken lips
were sewn. Where every man has taught us how to hate

each other. I look out the window
above the headboard, trade the pearls for

dawn at my throat, the peacock's beak sinking in
to my breast, drawing me against her iridescence.

Outside the rabbits chew and chew at the hill. Revolving
teeth plucking tuned pins. Beneath this blanket's lake

a body we've yet to recover.

OMPHALOS : CHRYSOPOEIA

Like all saints my mother had to unlearn obedience
with hunger. Nothing's without cost, even bruising rings into gold.
Days contract their indigo toward hunting season again

and I feed my mother coffee, cigarettes, and pears. She leaves
dragonflies by my bed at night, stills their emerald thrashing
with my help and fixes them in my hair, fills canvases

with my nape clasped by dead wings. I ask her how she's devoted
a life to the study of bright things with men in her bed
and she points to a nightingale singing in the pear tree

with a woman's voice though it has no tongue
now. *What kind of faith is this?* I ask, and she slips one finger
between my teeth, becomes water I swallow and hold

in my uterus. I stand before a canvas, shape I must unfold,
begin darkening the frame to escape through.

OMPHALOS : GNOSTIC

my mother kneels on the bed,
blonde hair falling around her girlbody
like a birch, and teaches the dark thought of me
in her the calm of naming colors:

        cerulean. trout-stocked
                lake. rattlesnake
           homed in rib. nitroglycerin
                    undone. antlered beauty.

all the things I must unlearn:
      harvesting spoons from dirt
      burning an umbilicus still milky in coils
      telling him he's such a good hunter
      telling myself to be quiet
      holding my breath in a frozen grove
          to keep from husking the ice off all the trees

OMPHALOS : HERESY

I come home to sleep against the smell of my mother's blood
and spit how men have told me to talk to them. *Mother I want*

to do something with anger. She hands me a throat and a cradle
     and I follow her to the sump pit at the center of the house

     behind her canvases. We each take turns spitting inside
until we have a flood. I say *mother I never fell in love* and she peels back

the flesh of her belly, shows me a red uterus studded with bone tines
     upon which to sharpen myself. When I was born I turned

     around and helped her give birth to herself. I say *mother I want*
to be seen and she sends me to gather quail feathers dropped across the winter

field after the cat, arranges them at home beside the heifer skull
     and tube of ochre. Says train your sight enough and you can crosshair anything

     alive. Rattlesnake bites and vaginal births can both be a reason
for a home burial. *Mother I want something good.* She tells me genesis

began with a woman offering her rib to all the hungry unnamed
     animals left in the wake of the words that set them moving.

     All the rest is just men's talk and hearsay.

OMPHALOS : EPOCH

Who taught you stars are just milk, sweating?
Who taught your body to unfold?

Behind the latched coal of your mouth
is the girl who pushed down the boy
who told you that you were not strong.

Today you do not have to feel nice.
You can barb yourself with disappointment
and the rachis of shoulder blades,
gnaw things at your wrists.

When you feel like a skinned heart
rest its blue thumping in a white cage.

Today all the men laugh and eat the churches
of your future empty, leave you to resuscitate charcoal
and chalk.

Rise up, small-bodied bone-girled thing,
remember the clicking of your body
into the chamber
of your mother's pelvis.

Remember the sentence you scavenged
in her, the granite flue you lived in
for years, teaching yourself to see.

The men undo the indigo ring
that haloes everyone's breathing.
Strand us without oxygen's caul.
Mangled shield. But you

have lived in the remains of chapel and hair,
draped yourself in another atmosphere

siphoned from your mother's blue skeleton.
Timbered casket, gray-bored
ache once called lungs.

Say this ash you've syrinxed
into something that can save. Sternum,
holy, word mineralized to blade.

OMPHALOS : SANCTUARY

Mother what a strange animal I am, how difficult
it is to be daughter. After the wedding is over

when the bride and groom and all the guests have gone
home, my friends and I are the ones who are left

locked in the church, running through the dark
with white veils moon enough to see by.

We drop on all fours, clutch the blue flowers
we've been thrown to remain single for good.

Waists wrapped in bone cords, we are the ace girls,
children of an uncertain season, sleeping in our clothes

at the foot of the altar and its cross, the deer
grazing our hair strung down the foramen's cracked pew.

Lord I have rarely believed enough in mothers
and sisters and friends. Pink snow falls across the mountains

beyond this long dark church
of the hips. How else could they be taught to bleed

at dawn, shed the most necessary thing? Mother
I kneel to be broken this way, trembling at the mouth

of the north. Hush me, now, fold and kiss me gently
back into your blood, press your lips

and knife to my throat, quiet me with feast.

OMPHALOS : RECESSIONAL

When I leave my mothers' house, it is with a wedding dress
      wrenching my shoulder like an augur each time I push it

still further down my grandmother's body, burying her
      mouth in my breast as I wrap her in lace and love letters

her mother kept from her. The stars brooched at her throat
      mares' eyes I plucked from the night. When I was born there was only

the sky slit neatly above me and a clean light, a way up
      instead of through, a plier-cut fence held open for me. I burn

my grandmother's body and sweep the ashes into a firwood box
      I tip into my mouth, swallow whole. Down the corridor I throw

up, step outside and into my mother on lengthening haunches
      and cloven hooves. My mouth a bow, my tongue an arrow

honey-loosened to its coarsest speech. My back uncorseted from moon
      I leap snow, each hoofprint curving from omega to lyre.

WE ARE CHANGED TO DEER AT THE BROKEN PLACE

and we all find our way here in time / to the house we've made of shame and bone /
to the hour of deer licking between our thighs / however you daughter / however you
drove back last night / up a highway toward a north you barely remember / along the
front range / and woke in this sprawled sheet of bed / rock you've always known in
the back of your skull / each of us has curled beneath the angel's cold wing / telling us
that you deserved this shame / and staggering into a sunrise / slatted pink across the
wall / through the curtains' dust your mother / remembered your body into this place
/ the way she pointed / to the line of does / cutting behind your house / saying look
/ so close to your cheek / the buck scraping the bark / from the tree you carved your
name into / and you who hated yourself / you who claimed to love others like you but
secretly despised / this life you were born into / have stepped out of it into a cleaner /
light startled by these bones you're coming into / heart a carnivorous ruby clenched
between your teeth / walking toward the sound of all the mothers who've guided you
this far / who gave you blood maybe / we can only carry some of this a little ways as
far as we can / and then give it to someone else / freeway sounds blown on a wind
off / a highway where nothing dies / and maybe we're tuning to a radio / dilated
open to something beautiful / something wise / a shelter in the curve of an on-ramp /
where we tread ground studded with antlers / picking our way strong enough to figure
out / how to carry / through mineral and hair and gasoline / and this voice quiet
in the static / psalms saying keep going / here you are forgiven / you who never did
anything wrong in the first place / by such femoral light / we lean to one another we
wound into each other's tender bones / kissing clavicles we split / and we are changed
to deer at the broken place / following a path to water

EPITHALAMIUM

you told me once that the world   is burning and people who believe
the bridegroom is coming want   to let it burn because this is not the world

you were up all last night   with a dog not your own, one arm wrapped around
the lightning   shaking shadows loose like spears again and again

I look at you on the floor   and the blanket is on fire
and I touch my hair and it is   on fire but I'm told that this is not the world

I tire of making a veil   I want to reveal this end this wall behind shadow to say
this body of mine loves you like a moth: mouthless, loves you all ways but that

let me fill your house with rain from the high country   let me fill it with sleep
let me fill your chest with toothed flowers   and stars for worship

if I make you the spaces between fibula   and tibia church doors twinned
pinebox coffins floated downstream   in pearls of coyote cries in throat

nothing but lace and bone   to chapel this distance
and nothing but a cross and a highway   to sternum this meat we survive on

what we'll make a home   out of what nearly killed us
that we made a bed of antlers and muscle   of men who tried to eat us

now made soft in their silence   so wholly removed from their former
appetites, their violent shapes   milded to such quiet forms

what do pears and tears have in common?   the smallest listening tucked inside
their wet flesh   if you cradle them in your palm

dust wings spiral into the blue votive candles   I can only open before you
pull me from the belly of a hound   and let me be the light you see by

let me save every animal   through the windows of your skin
let me pull everything home   through the blessing of your flesh

in the hot mothersleep   we all try to embrace
a small set of lungs   in a small set of ribs

ACTAEON

You stumbled here to look at this body, your ring clinking on the neck of the bottle dangling from your right hand, your left parting snowberry at the riverbank to see the hair, the breasts, the hips hitched to blue water's circles. Line of her back the bruisable sting of a cactus. Areoles scrubbed with current broken silver. Silt corset. You came here to bury your habits in the shore and wade to her bathing, to undo the faded sky of your jeans and lick her thighs, to taste mud's veil and gasp your name into the red nave until she was saved from a life without want. Teach her to be wanted, you to want. You were made of every man's hands, fashioned by saliva, desire, rust, power, this. I turn to see and change you into a blunt-muzzled hunger. Shattered into a furculum of tongues. Skin split by muscles overtaking your body, stones clattering beneath your cleaving hoofs as you outrun afternoon's gold and shuck your testicles between a different set of haunches. I make a myth of you to teach us all how to be something better. I take everything we excused you with—lust, libido, my body—and make it wordless. Each of us have carried you for a time, thought of you as our own, this god we have made inside all our bellies with each retelling: who was made to hunt, who to be hunted. With you we have set the table for the fathers to feast in unending line. I am making a new heart, blood-heavy and true behind the flushed blind of your nipples. I am trading your voice of brute godhead for a stag's clean thirst. I am setting you on a new path. The hounds that press close will not be strangers; the sky, familiar with teeth.

REFUGIA

This is the point where all waters divide
above gulch and canyon where gunpowder
was hidden before reservoir poured over the ghost

of a town where people now swim, stripped
to plunge where bone yokes water and glass
churning the skeletons of shad, spottail, cutthroat,

restocked each time they're hunted gone.
These are the remnants of all our
uses: condoms and brown-glass beer bottles, cigarette butts,

boot snug on blunted splinters of a snapped branch.
A rattlesnake coiled on a pink scrap of paper,
back broken across the wide-ruled lines

tongue welded to each word with blood—
I love this place so hard
it scares me. I came of age in the extinction.

Once I used to sink my wrists to the pulse
in cold streams prying up trilobites and cystoid stalks
fragile scallops I turned over and over on my palms

on the bank. Each dark wet
imprint of my hands soaking into
shale and basalt. I thumbed each asexual thing, let them teach me

the name for myself when no one else did. I developed other labels
for myself: *bird resurrecter, hell's starlight,*
breasts' orogeny, pinking lava dams slagged craters.

Blue-studded, strung-marrowed, fossil-belled—
I used to breathe a zero on the mirror.
Trace the tributary called the Virgin,

wonder about ventricles' jagged tectonics.
                                        I came out here

to breathe the clean ache of woods.

                                Another woman walked here to burn
everything he ever gave her: the letter, the shutter-
clicked photos—shedding each thing to arrive at the necessary

hunger. The fire that spread to the forest such a blaze
of wedding song, the singe-lunged birds unraveling
            the sky's white blank.

What we love, we must consume wholly.
                                What ash leaves in its wake
        unfurls slowly from bark, rock, hole,

                        such small shelters for the last hearts
of their kinds under such faithless glass.
                                From such

comes everything. May we find a way
                    to remember this. May we be
so spared.

RECITATIVE

Indigo buntings swell the birch with chittering male
voices under my ribs, each peck-singing *sweet baby how're you so*
perfect, weren't you made for me, where're you headed, do you live
alone, how do you know what you want if you haven't had a real man yet?

I reach under my breast to gently cup one's thrumming
and break its wing, pinch its fluttered tugging by its limp
limb's feathers, fling it against a wall, still its twisting.
From its cracked skull I pluck a seed, push it between

my teeth. Repeat this with each one till I have enough to survive
on all winter. When reddening weather warms their bones
tremble and I swallow their migration ache to north
the others with coverts tucked in hollow chests.

We don't owe anyone anything. In our laps we make a net of hair,
larkspur, spit. Turn each bird's plump rigging into shiver
to keep away cold. Beat skeletons to dough. Each beak's legible
puncture a pledge we make: resuscitate. Fletch. Covenant. Release.

Nights we blanket ourselves with its fledged ledger against frost-
rimmed stars. Days, catch a wind to something better.

AROMANTIC / ASEXUAL

I rise at the pale hour   drowning in daylight
                    that's leaked through windows
          forgotten, unlatched   rain blowing in.
                                                  Barefoot on the honeywood floors
                    I pass the photograph of the bridge   arching its rusting back
                         in the living room   offering a way to shelter—
                                             cross running water
                              and a spirit will stop chasing you
but it is the bedroom door I have chosen to leave
               behind   an empty bed does not   haunt me.

                    I learn to lung this wet, this roof
          think of my mother telling me
                                   if you ever wanted an abortion
                         I would take you there   *not drag you to church.*

          I could mistake night detaching from utility wires
                         for a bird   I want bark to suckle   to hold me close.

     What am I supposed to want?
                         I bow to the zipper in the wooden floorboards
               undo it with my teeth   hoping for hunger to make   me whole
                                   but out erupt magnolia trees
          and paper birch, pink petals
                         and salmon spilling   coining the new air
                    unhinging the ceiling.

I walk out between narrow corridors of trees   everything moss and blossom
                    unmarrowed and bitten I wade
                         into the slate water   of the river
               wonder if the fish still cut their bodies through
                              this current.

I would support you
if it's what you wanted

72

I lower my hands into the green   wonder if it is the moss I am
wanting if breast if church   if death
        what I am   blossoming
                          I feel the many hungers of fish
        beneath the drown of surface and cloud.

I will   turn my palms up and let something
                wriggle from my spine   this promise of teeth
                    milt, milk seeping into water
                          leading us all into the new after.

CONVERSION WITH PETRICHOR AND THIS CLITORIS

Somewhere west of Maroon Bells and the hardest part of my
body I pull over and put the parking brake on. Gravel and sunrise
brittle underfoot, scattered with the things I've made a life out of
up until now: the nail all the iron in me could be reduced to, hip
bones clawed with ice, six days from blood and the bits of shame
I've let build up in my body against my best intentions. I swore
I'd never be that person but here I am looking over my shoulder,
checking for headlights that might've followed me up the winding
road to the middle of my life so far, this canyon road of yawning
stone. Morning of coffee, boot, and a black wing's tremble. Truck
light and rust and maybe something good. Clavicle and a cold
forge. I came out here to remind myself—something about
belief and my body. Speak the names of those like me, girls gone
underworld, into the mouths of rattlesnakes. Watch how their
hearts turn in their bodies, stones.

/

We were saved,
mother, for the men
we were to give ourselves to.
Lean years when bucks
rubbed velvet against the Ford
rusting its skeleton in the field and girlbodies
needled with such gold
barn dust and hay stilled in doorways.
What man would not have lost his salvation
in me, brief as November's indigo,
in the unchapeled shadows
of truckbed and my skull.

/

Don't be temptation.
Don't be coyote and hunting

season, fall
-en woman. Don't be a man
don't love anything
but his hair's slow creek
-spun sunlight, unbodied.

Unholy conjugation:
She deserved
He deserved
They deserved
God deserves
The godly deserve
The fallen deserve
Devil deserved

Semis parked in fields scrawled with red paint: *pray an end to abortion.*

/

I laid myself down on the bed beneath winter's cross
-hairs of light, threshold at which I've cupped my lips
again and again—
in my small room I took what was meant for them
and gave it to myself
a dark so full of my heartbeat
I thought I was a horse
lulled in grace, rocking my softening pelvic bone
against my hand taut pearling
under the white sheet
and the ceiling light's mouth-drowned
tungsten begging my name.
This secret satisfaction I carried for days knowing what I had denied
men. And meanwhile all the mothers bowed
their heads and prayed over their children
walking into the winter fields

may they be saved, saved, saved.

/

Nothing escapes punishment forever. Here is the thaw; here, her
bones returned at the base of the cliff, used. I come out here
ready to shed everything, let go of the false things I've believed—
men's hands, tongues, the necessary burning of this place—and
to remember wire, snow runoff, toughened breasts. Lord, mother,
I came out here to be made whole and clean again. Forgive each
time his voice has called to me across the street and I've said
nothing. Each time he's asked if I'm single, if I live alone while
he's driving me home, if I know I have snow on my boots and I
kept my fist inside my throat. Each time I've doubted the story
told to me by a friend about his hands. Each time I've wanted to
wrench something loose from the mineral lake behind my ribs.
Take this heart of flesh and give me something stronger. I came
out here to remind myself of the truth of clitoris, lip, force, cold.
Lord, I vow to speak in cold air the shape they tried to reduce me
to: *cunt, cunt, cunt.*

I'll praise the labia dark as gun muzzle:
           bearded capshell, doe lips nuzzling charred calayxes.

Praise hip and obturator foramen
           clotting with avalanche lilies thick as bottle necks.

Praise the slicked ligament and churned lining
           belly-held above my thighs, the memory of water
           locked the way rock layers hold lake: I'm silt-wave
                       knocking in the absent heart
                                   of a fish's skeleton.

I'm struck iron.
           Eucharist torn up

to feed the starving crows. Coverts and arched back.
               I'm roughed brown feathers over the pink chapel doors.

I spit my molars into the ground
and each one grows a new girl
I raise to know the strength of their body
and to take the kick of the cold stock
of their anger.
                  I can touch myself into a winter morning
and it will never be for anyone.
       I'm rainbow riffled round the edges of oil puddle. Caudal tail
and travesty. I'm so beautiful
I can't stop licking my own name.
                     I'll reach down
to grab the hands of every unbreathed girlbody
trapped underground beneath me. Pull each up
from my chest
          to follow my tracks back across the whitened field,
our bodies swallowing themselves into winter sky.

WHERE THE RIB TAKES ROOT

I return to the place where I was first undone.
For years I've carried this stone baby
behind the locked nest of my pubic bone.
Little prisoner, calcified twin
I could not birth
no matter how hard I tried
to pretend I didn't winter it
in its little box, brute season
after brute season. When I was old enough
to be daughter I wrenched free
of my mother's hips and fled across
the back of another set of days. This skull
between my thighs I could not
be rid of. Womb's snowmelt
unyoking every house I thrashed to
and tried to plant a prairie in.
I've spit on my mothers' names
blamed them for what hands did to us
rocked and rocked in this umbilicus
of galvanized steel and mud, palms
snowing open. There was so much I could
not forgive my mother for. This cursed life. This anger
I didn't know what to do with.
How we didn't know how to be mothered.
Men devour the ash they root inside women.
And now when I come home
crawling across the wind, I drag my breasts
over these sharpened antlers, this hush
of night's indigo draping round my shoulders.
Baby. Baby. In the cold my mother's voice

                              tells me through the snake in the story
you are not a bad person. Arsenic
                              lives at the core of knowledge
and if you eat it slowly over years
                              you can build strength enough for anything.
I've sucked these seeds I stole from beneath
                              the ground, remembered how to be strong,
daughter cell after daughter cell pounding
                              this queer heart of mine into its blue shape.
The deer here hang
                              from floorboards and drain for three days
until they're emptied enough to walk free.
                              In the darkroom under the house
among the wet red negatives I cradle
                              my mother between my thighs
to help us give birth.
                              Massage the c-section scar where I was sliced
with such violence from her body.
                              Tell her there is no shame. Tell her
we can be daughters again together—including me, a them.
                              Headwatered in these bodies of ours.
Something blasphemes through us
                              with a howl of such practiced thirst.

ACKNOWLEDGMENTS

Grateful acknowledgment is made to the editors of the following publications in which some of these poems first appeared, sometimes in alternate versions:

Blue Mesa Review: "Crown of Screws," selected by Eduardo Corral as the winner of the 2020 Poetry Contest
Gertrude Press: "Devil's Rope, Winter's Testament" (with gratitude for Stephanie Glazier and the editors' nomination for a Pushcart Prize)
Hobart: "Nocturne with Aroace Girl"
The Journal: "Aroace Girl, Leveed," "Where the Sky's Milk Comes In"
The Laurel Review: "What the Water Bruises Us Into," "Omphalos : Sanctuary," "Omphalos : Recessional"
The Missouri Review: "Actaeon"
Mud Season Review: "Asexual / Aromantic"
Pacifica Literary Review: "Omphalos : Epoch"
Palette Poetry: "when I learned to be fourteen"
Passages North: "North of Hell"
Perhappened: "Aro Ace Girl's Petition"
Pidgeonholes: "Omphalos : Heresy"
Pithead Chapel: "We Are Changed to Deer at the Broken Place"
Qu: "Aroace Girl with Traps"
Ruminate: "Aubade with Aroace Girl" (originally published as "Aubade with Aro Ace Woman")
Southeast Review: "Conversion with Petrichor and This Clitoris"
South Florida Poetry Journal: "Omphalos : Termed," "Omphalos : Shorn"
Sycamore Review: "Nuptial Bones"
Tinderbox: "Reasons I Wouldn't Be a Good Mother," "Where the Rib Takes Root"
Tupelo Quarterly: "Aroace Girl : Plainsong Elegy," "Abstinence"
Yalobusha Review: "little song, quickening," "Aroace Girl with Kettles and Cradles"

The closing lines of "Aroace Girl, Leveed" re-uses / remixes closing lines of my poem "Jeremiad with Dead Foxes and Blackbird Songs," which originally appeared in *Fourth River*.

Gratitude, gratitude, gratitude. Gratitude to Tupelo Press for choosing this book, which still overwhelms me with joy every day, and to the entire editorial team for their kindness, stewardship, and ushering of this book into the world. To Kristina Marie Darling, Jeffrey Levine, David Rossitter, and all of the others who have worked so hard on making this book what it is—what a dream it's been to get to work with all of you. To the editors of all the journals in which these poems first appeared, with special thanks to Emma Bolden, for seeing something in my work at Tupelo

Quarterly and for the wonderful conversation that has grown as a result. To Chelsea Dingman and Carol Guess, for holding this book in their hands so gently and with so much generosity while I continue to be in such awe of them.

To the people who read the first poems that became this book at the Bread Loaf Environmental Writers Conference, including workshop instructor Sean Hill, for seeing something inside them and breathing courage into them. To Lucien Darjeun Meadows and the conversation and friendship that grew out of that conference. To Jose Hernandez Diaz, John James, Susannah Lodge-Rigal, Kristin McIntyre, and Candelin Wahl and the editorial staff at Mud Season for their incredible insight and feedback as these poems grew into a book. Without you, this book would not be here.

To my Colorado State University thesis advisors, mentors, classmates, friends—thank you for helping me become not only the writer I am, but the community we are a part of, continuing to learn together. To all of you for your brilliance, your kindness, your friendship, your poems and your essays and your stories on the wet grass in autumn and coffee cups shared together. You are all the poem in my life. And to Stephanie G'Schwind, for teaching us all what community looks like on and off the pages of a book and a journal, for guiding me and so many others into this wide and beautiful world of letters.

To Margaret Browne and Michelle Thomas, whose love and friendship and stunning writing continue to crack me wide open. May there always be a kitchen table (and cats) at the center of the three of us. May we always have reading to each other and giggling on the floor, sharing words and homemade marshmallows and queer movie nights. To Stephanie Hempel and Derek Pufahl, for house plants, tea, foxes in the fields, your gorgeous writing. For your support of this book and all of your help bringing it out into the world and for bringing me back to center. For all the light streaming out of our bones together on road trips through the mountains, sing where the radio and cell phone tower signals do not reach. So far from where we lived in Nebraska and yet all still together. To Abby and the wind we carry in our ribs, for teaching me to live the most honest and loving life possible. To all the years and miles and roads we've carried with us in our friendship. To Sasha, Gordon, Bill, Sara, Shannon, Liz, Erin, Elly, Jennie, Alie, Brandon, and this particularly lovely community we've made together—thank you for your hearts, your support, your particular ways of showing up in the world every single day and astounding me all over again with your wit and warmth.

To all the writers and mentors in Colorado, Nebraska, Missouri and beyond who have taught me, shaped me, written alongside me, made space for me, encouraged me, showed me how to find a home and teeth in words before my hands even knew how to carry it all. With special thanks to JV and all the horses. To all the visiting writers, workshop friends, teachers. Breath and bone, all of you, thank you. I'm only here because of each of you.

To my parents, the first artists in my life, for all of your love and support and encouragement to keep writing and keep finding a life in words, for coming to all the readings. Thanks for showing me how to create, in every way possible.

And lastly to you. For creating a little space in your body for this book. You're what the poem has made, is making. Keep going.

NOTES

Some of these poems are in conversation with other poems or texts:

Two of the italicized lines in "Gold Shyness" use language from Anne Carson's *Eros the Bittersweet*.

The italicized words in "Orienting" come from Nadia Nooreyezdan's article "Asexuality is a Sexual Orientation, Not a Disorder" in *The Swaddle*: "In 2016, researchers at the University of British Columbia published a paper concluding that asexuality is not a psychiatric condition or a disorder, but a distinct sexual orientation."

The ampersand image in "Aroace Girl with Traps" is a reference to something Eduardo Corral mentioned in a reading I heard him give; he, in turn, said Brenda Hillman had drawn the comparison between an ampersand and a pregnant woman doing yoga. This is also referenced in "On the Ampersand: Eduardo C. Corral" in *The Whole Garden Will Bow*: https://thewholegardenwillbow.wordpress.com/2011/12/09/on-the-ampersand-eduardo-c-corral/

"Asexual / Aromantic" is in conversation with zipper imagery in both Corral's poem "Want" in *Slow Lightning* and sam sax's poem "Phonomania: A History of Noise," from the latter's book *bury it*. The line "am I not animal enough for you" in "Aubade with Aroace Woman" was partly inspired by/is a response to a similar line in Corral's "To the Angelbeast," and "Omphalos : Sinkbox" is indebted to Corral's poem "Watermark."

The title "Conversion with Petrichor and this Clitoris" was partly inspired by the title of Webster's poem "Conversion Narrative" in her book *The Trailhead*. The title of "Where the Sky's Milk Comes In" was partly inspired by the two closing lines of Webster's "This is Manifest," also in *The Trailhead*.

The refrain in "Aroace Girl : Plainsong Elegy" was partly inspired by Chelsea Dingman's "Testimony of Hinges" from *Thaw*.

The poem "Dermatillomania" was partly influenced by Cassandra J. Bruner's "Fugue with a Procession of Visitors."

I'm grateful to the many contemporary writers who are grappling with mother-daughter / child themes, particularly Lidia Yuknavitch, Maggie Smith, Rachel McKibbens, Natalie Scenters-Zápico, Margaret Browne, Kristin McIntyre, and Sasha Steensen, all of whose work has pushed me directly or indirectly to keep thinking about these relationships and have had some form of influence across this work in what I hope is a conversation.

To the many writers I've been influenced by over the years, including both my lovely friends in my immediate writing community and the authors I've encountered whose influence I don't even fully recognize: thank you, thank you, thank you.